IN THEIR OWN WORDS

Betsy Ross

Especially for Martha. Your love of life and family is exemplary.
Plus, you keep us in stitches!

ACKNOWLEDGMENTS

The authors would like to acknowledge the fine folks of the Independence National Historical Park for all of their information, insights, and help. Thank you also to the welcoming worshippers of Christ Church. They would especially like to thank Cheri Holt of the Carpenters' Company of Philadelphia for her enthusiasm and interest.

Great thanks and appreciation go to Dr. Whitney Smith of the Flag Research Center. His insights and ideas contributed much to the accuracy of this book.

LIBRARY OF CONGRESS CATALOGING-IN-PUBLICATION DATA
Roop, Connie.
Betsy Ross/Connie Roop and Peter Roop
p. cm.—(In their own words)
Includes bibliographical references and index.
1. Ross, Betsy, 1752–1836—Juvenile literature.   2. Revolutionaries—United States—Biography—Juvenile literature.   3. United States—History—Revolution, 1775–1783—Flags—Juvenile literature.   4. Flags—United States—History—18th century—Juvenile literature. [1. Ross, Betsy, 1752–1836.   2. United States—History—Revolution, 1775–1783—Biography.   3. Revolutionaries.   4. Flags—United States.   5. Women—Biography.]   I. Ross, Betsy, 1752–1836.   II. Roop, Peter.   III. Title.
IV. In their own words (Scholastic)
E302.6.R77 R66 2001
973.3'092—dc21   00-066139

ISBN 0-439-26321-2

10 9 8 7 6 5 4   02 03 04 05

Composition by Brad Walrod
Printed in the U.S.A.
First printing, November 2001

CONTENTS

INTRODUCTION

"RESOLVED—THAT THE FLAG OF THE United States be 13 stripes alternate red and white, that the Union be 13 stars white in a blue field representing a new constellation."

This sentence from the *Journals of Congress*, June 14, 1777, describes the design of the first official flag of the new United States. Not even a year old, the young nation needed a flag for its armies and navy. Various flags had flown during early battles of the American Revolution. By 1777, though, General George Washington and Congress believed one flag was needed to display our country's unity.

How then did Betsy Ross, credited with creating the first flag, gain that fame? Did she really sew a flag in June of 1776, a full year before Congress described a United States flag?

No written documents are left to tell Betsy's actual story. She didn't leave any letters describing her famous flag. She didn't keep a diary.

Later in her life, Betsy's relatives listened to her tell of meeting George Washington. They said she told about making the very first American flag and how she improved Washington's flag design. She suggested the thirteen stars have only five points, instead of the six points Washington wanted.

How do we know this?

In fact, Betsy Ross's role in making the flag was unknown until her grandson, William J. Canby, gave a speech about her in 1870. In his talk, Canby told how he heard his grandmother, Betsy Griscom Ross Ashburn Claypoole (she married three times), frequently tell of meeting General Washington. Canby detailed how she came to create the American flag.

Canby spent days in Washington, D.C., reading the official records of the American Revolution. He wanted to find written proof of her story, but he couldn't. Betsy's role in making the first flag was not mentioned anywhere. Other descendants of Betsy Ross, however, signed documents swearing Betsy told them about the flag.

Sophia Hildebrande, Betsy's granddaughter, wrote, "I remember to have heard my grandmother, Elizabeth Claypoole [Betsy Ross], frequently narrate the circumstances of her having made the first Star Spangled Banner."

A niece wrote, "I, Margaret Boggs, of the City of Philadelphia, widow, do hereby certify that I have heard my aunt, Elizabeth Claypoole, say many times that she made the first Star Spangled Banner that was ever made."

What then is the true story? Did Betsy Ross make the first American flag or not? Today, history is not clear one way or the other. There are no records of her making the first flag.

We do know someone made the first Stars and

No portraits of Betsy Ross were made during her lifetime. So no one knows exactly what she looked like. Here is one portrait of Betsy. It is based on written descriptions of her.

Stripes. Maybe that someone was Betsy Ross. In 1776, she had the skills, the materials, and the knowledge to make flags. She knew General Washington. She was a loyal patriot, a person who took the side of the thirteen colonies in their disagreements with the British.

Many people have researched the life of Betsy Ross. Betsy Ross was skilled with needle and thread. She ran her own upholstery business covering chairs, making curtains, and stitching tablecloths. Documents show she made flags in May 1777. She continued to sew flags for another fifty years.

Betsy lived most of her life in Philadelphia, Pennsylvania, the first capital of the United States. Philadelphia was the scene of many important events in early U.S. history. In 1836, she died there in the home of her daughter, Jane Canby. Jane's son, William, told his grandmother's story long after her death.

Piecing together Betsy Ross's life is like creating a quilt. Each separate piece from various sources has to be stitched together to make the whole picture.

Because we do not have Betsy's words, we must find out about her life from other sources.

Some people write diaries about their lives. Others enjoy writing letters to friends and families. George Washington wrote thousands of letters and army orders. Christopher Columbus kept journals. It is through sources like these that we learn about the daily life and adventures of people long ago.

We call diaries and letters primary sources. A primary source is the actual account of a person's experiences. A letter from Eleanor Roosevelt, the autobiography of Ben Franklin, and a journal by Lewis and Clark are primary sources.

Using a primary source is like listening to someone tell a personal story in his or her own words. It is the closest we can come to an event that actually happened. A videotape, your diary, and a photograph from a family celebration are all examples of modern primary sources.

Much of what we know about Betsy Ross and her life comes from secondary sources. A secondary source is information about an event or a life recorded by someone who was not an eyewitness. A biography by a descendant of Betsy Ross is a secondary source. An entry in an encyclopedia is also a secondary source. This biography is a secondary source, although it does have quotes from primary sources.

In this book we used primary sources to describe Betsy Ross's life and times. We also used many secondary sources to learn about her and the world in which she lived. Through both types of sources, it is possible to piece together the quilt of Betsy Ross's life. In doing so, we share her story so you can decide whether she actually made the first flag of the United States.

Whether or not Betsy Ross created the first flag, her life reflects the birth of the United States. She was an eyewitness to many of the events that shaped our country.

Through her life and the words of others living at the time, we can glimpse our early history as a nation.

CHAPTER 2

BETSY'S BIRTH

JANUARY 1, 1752, DAWNED COLD AND clear in Philadelphia, Pennsylvania. It was the first day of the first month of the new year. A newborn baby cried in her mother's arms. The baby girl, Elizabeth, was Samuel and Rebecca Griscom's ninth child.

Her parents named her Elizabeth, but she was soon called Betsy. Today, we know her best as Betsy Ross.

When Elizabeth was born on January 1, 1752, there was no United States. Instead, there were the thirteen British colonies in America: Massachusetts, New Hampshire, New York, Connecticut, Rhode Island, Pennsylvania, New

Jersey, Delaware, Maryland, Virginia, North Carolina, South Carolina, and Georgia.

No one knew the enormous changes America and Philadelphia would experience during her lifetime. No one could have predicted the role Betsy Ross would play in those changes.

Betsy's father, Samuel Griscom, was a carpenter and builder. Like his father and grandfather before him, Samuel built houses and buildings in the rapidly growing region at the head of Delaware Bay.

In 1751, just before Betsy was born, Samuel helped build the first belfry on the Pennsylvania State House. Samuel also helped construct Friends Meeting House, where the Quaker Griscom family worshipped. His talented hands helped build numerous other buildings in and around Philadelphia. Some of these sturdy buildings with thick brick walls and strong oak beams still stand in Philadelphia today.

Betsy's great-grandfather, Andrew Griscom, arrived in America in 1680. He found a beautiful wilderness. This land, called Pennsylvania or Penn's

The belfry—or bell tower—of the Pennsylvania State House can be seen in the upper right-hand corner of this picture. Today, this famous building is called Independence Hall.

Woods, was owned by William Penn, a rich Englishman. Penn was given 45,000 square miles of land as a reward for helping the English king.

Penn's Woods provided the first English settlers with animals for food and wood for building. There was no sawmill for cutting trees into boards, so the first settlers dug holes into the steep banks of the

Delaware River for their homes. These "cave" homes stretched for a half mile along the river. After the first winter, trees were chopped down and log cabins built.

William Penn was a member of the Society of Friends, better known as the Quakers. One of the first log buildings was the Friends Meeting House, a Quaker place of worship. The Quakers were strong believers in the education of both boys and girls. The second largest cabin became the Quaker school.

Penn called his settlement Philadelphia, or the "City of Brotherly Love." He wanted his city "to promote good Discipline and just government among a plain and well-intending people." William Penn said all religions that worshipped God would be welcome in Philadelphia.

Betsy's great-grandfather, Andrew Griscom, bought nearly 500 acres of land. He and his neighbors had plenty of trees for lumber. To the settlers' delight, clay was found in the ground. This clay made perfect bricks.

With a cheap supply of wood and bricks, Philadelphia quickly grew. Builders like the Griscoms were in demand and made a good living. Soon the village became a city spreading across the two miles between the Delaware River on the east and the Schuylkill River on the west.

Remembering the many trees they first found in the area, Philadelphians named their streets Pine, Walnut, Spruce, Locust, and Chestnut.

By 1752, when Betsy was born, Philadelphia was the largest city in America. More than 20,000 people walked its streets and bought supplies in its shops. Industrious citizens, like Benjamin Franklin, contributed to Philadelphia's wealth and prosperity.

Philadelphia was located in the middle of the thirteen original colonies. With easy access to the sea, the city became a trading center for all of the colonies. Wheat, wood, flour, and other American products were shipped to England and Europe. Cotton cloth, iron, paper, pottery, sugar, silk, books, guns, linen, and other goods were bought from British merchants.

Thus it was in the busy, bustling city of Philadelphia that Betsy Griscom was to grow up, marry, run her own business, and raise a family.

A large family was commonplace during colonial times. Over the years, Samuel and Rebecca had seventeen children. Unfortunately, not every child lived to be an adult. Many colonial children died from yellow fever, smallpox, measles, and whooping cough. Elizabeth Drinker, who lived near Betsy, wrote in 1762, "A Sickley time at Philadelphia. Many Persons are taken down with something very like the Yellow-Fever." This epidemic lasted from August until October. Betsy was ten.

Accidents also claimed many lives. Children drowned. Houses burned. Boats sank.

Only nine Griscom children lived to be adults— one boy and eight girls, including Betsy, survived.

The large house in which Betsy was born had been built by her grandfather. He later moved across the Delaware River to New Jersey. Samuel and Rebecca moved into his Philadelphia home with their growing family. Before long, Samuel built his

The Liberty Bell's last true note was heard on February 22, 1846 —George Washington's birthday. On that day the bell's famous crack was formed.

own home on Arch Street.

During 1752, Betsy's first year, two exciting events happened. In June, Benjamin Franklin flew his kite and discovered electricity. In August, a new bell arrived from England. It was to be hung in the State House belfry that young Betsy's father had helped build.

On September 1, 1752, Isaac Norris of Philadelphia wrote, "The Bell is come ashore and in good order...'tho we have not tryed [tried] the sound."

Inscribed on the bell's base were these words, "Proclaim Liberty thro' all the Land to all the Inhabitants."

The bell sometimes rang announcing important events. Betsy heard it toll many times during her long life in Philadelphia.

Today, this famous bell is called the Liberty Bell.

CHILDHOOD

BETSY'S CHILDHOOD WAS BUSY. SHE attended Quaker Meetings to worship on Sundays and Thursdays. She took care of her younger brothers and sisters.

There were never-ending chores. Meals were cooked and dishes washed. The woodbox was filled and garden tended. Beds were made and floors swept.

Wool was spun into yarn and the yarn woven into cloth. Betsy and her mother and sisters made their own clothes. Clothes also had to be mended. Betsy's small fingers became quite skillful with thread and needle.

Betsy was raised as a Quaker. The Quakers believed in living a simple life. Their furniture was plain and useful, not decorated.

Quaker clothes were simple, too. Betsy wore a gray dress, a white apron, and a white bonnet. Betsy's mother and sisters dressed the same way. Her father and brothers also dressed in plain clothes.

The Quakers frowned upon games, music, and cards. They did not dance. Reading was important, especially the Bible. Few Quakers read

Quakers, like this man from Pennsylvania, chose to dress in plain clothing.

novels or storybooks. One Quaker wrote, "There ought to be in every family some good books to be always at hand."

Sundays, or First Day as the Quakers called it, were set aside for prayer, attending Meeting, and reading the Bible. If the weather was nice, Sunday afternoons might also mean a walk in a park. Wealthy Quakers sometimes went for boat rides.

On First Day, Quakers gathered at Meeting Houses like this one in Philadelphia.

Elizabeth Drinker did this but felt uncomfortable. She wrote, "I do not like such doings on a First Day." So she walked home instead!

Betsy's parents set a good example for their children. They worked hard, went to Meeting twice a week, were thrifty, and loved their large family.

The Quaker Book of Discipline said, "Parents should be exemplary to their children in Conversation, and in keeping out of vain Fashions,

Customs, and Pride of the World, by adorning [dressing] themselves modestly and in Plainest [clothes]."

The Griscoms did enjoy picnics. In winter, they skated on the frozen river or went sledding. When Betsy was thirteen, the Delaware River froze solid. One day an ox was roasted on the ice. Imagine the fun the people had skating, laughing, and feasting on the frozen river.

With so many brothers and sisters, there was always someone to play with when the lively Betsy had time.

In colonial days few girls went to school. They stayed home to do the chores. Betsy's parents, however, believed all their children should know the Three R's: Reading, Writing, and Arithmetic.

When she was six years old, Betsy went to Rebecca Jones's home for her elementary schooling. Mrs. Jones lived at 8 Drinker's Alley, a few blocks from Betsy's home. Here Betsy learned to read, write, and do her sums. Betsy also had the opportunity to improve her sewing.

Before long, it was noticed that Betsy was skilled in sewing. It was something she enjoyed very much.

When Betsy outgrew Mrs. Jones's instruction, she went to the Friends Public School near the State House. William Penn set up the Friends Public School so "proper care might be taken about the learning and instruction of youth."

Here Betsy made new friends, some of whom were not Quakers. Although a Quaker school, Friends allowed children of any religion to attend. Many of Philadelphia's wealthiest citizens sent their children to the Friends Public School. Here, Susan Claypoole became one of Betsy's lifelong friends. Her brother, John Claypoole, also attended.

Betsy went to school from Monday to Friday and a half day on Saturday. She would walk to school in the morning and was in her seat when the State House bell rang at eight o'clock. She stayed until noon when she had two hours for dinner and exercise. At two o'clock Betsy was back until five.

Betsy followed this schedule as written for Quaker schools. "The scholars [should] be kept in the morning two hours at reading, writing, bookkeeping." After dinner, the afternoon was spent "two hours at reading, writing, etc." For the remaining time, the students worked on skills of their own choosing. The Quakers believed that students should spend this time practicing "that art, mystery or trade that he or she most delighteth in."

Betsy chose to perfect her skills with needle and thread. Someday, these same skills would bring her fame as well.

APPRENTICESHIP

IN 1764, WHEN BETSY WAS TWELVE, HER father decided her sewing skills should be used differently. He felt Betsy, though a girl, should learn a trade. Few girls or women held jobs outside their homes during colonial days. In a time when many women became widows at an early age, Mr. Griscom believed that if Betsy had a skill that earned money, she could support herself if she had to.

After all, Betsy's great-aunt Sarah, a talented seamstress, had once had her own business. She made "body linings" (corsets) and underclothes. Now in her seventies, Aunt Sarah lived with the Griscoms. She watched Betsy's younger brothers and sisters. She made new clothes for the

Griscoms and mended old clothes. Aunt Sarah shared her sewing expertise with Betsy, who was determined to become an excellent seamstress like her aunt.

Betsy admired her strong-willed aunt. Once, when a customer refused to pay his bill, Aunt Sarah had his name printed in a newspaper. The embarrassed man soon paid his bill!

Philadelphia in 1764 was a thriving city. Dozens of ships were being built in docks lining the Delaware River. All day, shipbuilders hammered and sawed. Sail makers cut and stitched great canvas sails. Rope makers twisted miles of new rope. Hundreds of ships carried products into and out of the city.

Farmers from the fertile region around Philadelphia came to town to sell and trade their products: butter, cheese, fruits, meats, vegetables, honey, and milk. They bought goods from shopkeepers to take home. Trappers bartered their bales of furs from the western wilderness.

Many merchants and shopkeepers were becoming

wealthy. Some families built country houses outside of town. There they spent the summer months avoiding the heat, dirt, and disease of crowded Philadelphia. One young girl wrote after a time in the country, "Don't call me a country girl. I pride myself on being a Philadelphian."

More money meant more people could afford expensive items like books, silk clothes, fine upholstered furniture, carpets, rich foods, linen tablecloths, and other luxuries.

Betsy's father kept busy building new homes, warehouses, churches, and shops. His business did well. Being a thrifty Quaker, he did not spend his hard-earned money on fancy things. Besides, he had just finished building his own new home on Arch Street. He had little money to spare.

So Betsy's schooling ended when she was twelve. She would become an apprentice.

In colonial times, apprentices worked for someone for free. Usually, they did this for five or more years. They apprenticed to learn a skill or a trade. Their masters taught them the business as

Benjamin Franklin and his partner opened their own print shop in 1728. The following year, Franklin became the publisher of The Pennsylvania Gazette, *a Philadelphia newspaper.*

well as providing food and lodging.

Benjamin Franklin had been a printer's apprentice. Later, he opened his own printing shop in Philadelphia. Other apprentices learned carpentry, shipbuilding, glassblowing, bricklaying, cabinet and furniture making, blacksmithing, and many other skilled trades. A hardworking apprentice hoped to open his own shop, prosper, and have his own apprentices someday.

Betsy's father felt that because she had such excellent sewing skills, she should work in an upholstery shop. She could live at home while learning the upholstery craft.

There were dozens of upholstery shops in Philadelphia in 1764. An upholsterer sewed fabric on chairs and then stuffed the fabric with horsehair, feathers, grass, or moss to make a comfortable seat. Homes like the Griscoms' still had only hard wooden furniture. But the rich people of Philadelphia wanted more comfort. They could afford it.

Upholsterers also made carpets, mattresses, and venetian blinds. They fashioned tablecloths, bed coverings, and blankets. They sewed drapes and bed hangings. The best upholsterers helped design entire homes from the carpets to the chair coverings to the drapes. Others might design and make one or two rooms for their customers.

Upholsterers also sewed flags for the ships sailing out of Philadelphia.

Betsy's father wanted her to work for a Quaker upholsterer. Mr. Griscom asked his Quaker friend John Webster if Betsy could apprentice at his upholstery shop. Mr. Webster knew Betsy. One day, when she was in his shop, she had helped one of his workers with a difficult piece of sewing. Mr. Webster was impressed.

Betsy became an apprentice at Webster's Upholstery Shop. She was eager to use her sewing skills. There were other apprentices at the shop, so first Betsy ran errands, swept the workroom floors, and carried supplies. Mr. Webster kept his fabrics, spare needles, canvas straps, brass nails, chair stuffings, extra tools, and other items in his cellar. Betsy, being the youngest apprentice, hurried up and down the steep stairs bringing the other workers what they needed.

In time Mr. Webster put her sewing skills to work. First, Betsy laid out patterns. Next, she learned how to cut silk, canvas, or linen fabrics for blankets, bed curtains, and chairs. She began basting, then stitching curtains, mattresses, drapes, and blankets.

The skills Betsy learned from her mother and aunt made her one of Webster's best apprentices. She enjoyed the work, her nimble fingers sewing all day. She also liked the many beautiful fabrics imported from England.

In early America, girls who were learning to sew made needlepoint samplers like this one.

At this time almost everything in the colonies was brought from England or its other colonies around the world. The English bought raw materials from the colonies, carried them to England, and sold finished things back to the colonists at a high price.

It was against the law for the American colonists to buy goods from other countries. The silk the colonists wanted went from China to England, then to America. The same with tea from India or linen from Ireland.

In 1765, to help pay the expense of keeping an army in America, the British added a tax to many goods sold in America. These taxes caused problems between England and its colonies. Many Americans did not want to pay these taxes. They complained they had no representation in Parliament in

London, which passed the taxes. The colonists felt that the taxes were unfair.

While colonists worried about growing problems with Britain, daily life kept them busy at home.

One apprentice in Mr. Webster's shop was a determined young man named John Ross. John was not a Quaker. He belonged to the Church of England. His father was a minister at Christ Church, one of the tallest and most beautiful buildings in town. *The Pennsylvania Gazette* newspaper wrote that Christ Church "in point of elegance surpasses everything of its kind in America."

Betsy often passed Christ Church on her way to the market. Little did she know what role this church would play in her life.

John Ross did not want to follow his father into the ministry. He dreamed of someday owning his own upholstery shop. To master the trade, he apprenticed at Webster's Upholstery Shop.

There he worked for years with Betsy Griscom. He admired her excellent sewing as well as her brown hair and dancing blue eyes. He also enjoyed her quiet confidence in herself. Betsy liked John, too. He was tall, handsome, and had good business sense.

Like Betsy, John had grown up in a large family. Many of his brothers and sisters died young. He had worn mended clothes. He knew the value of hard work and self-confidence.

With so much in common, Betsy Griscom and John Ross fell in love.

Both felt their parents would be against their marriage, so Betsy and John decided to elope. They would run away, get married, return, and open up their own upholstery shop.

MARRIAGE

JOHN AND BETSY WERE RIGHT. THEIR
parents opposed their plans for marriage. It
was against Quaker rules for Betsy to marry
someone who was not a Quaker. They called this
"marrying out of Meeting."

Betsy's parents took the matter to the Quaker
Meeting. Betsy was warned not to marry outside
her religion. If she would admit her mistake,
however, she could remain a Quaker.

Betsy refused. She loved John Ross and was
determined to spend her life with him. She had
turned twenty-one and could legally marry. John
was twenty-two years old.

On Thursday, November 4, 1773, Betsy and
John eloped. They knew they could not marry in

Former First Lady Dolley Madison belonged to the Society of Friends in Philadelphia until she married James Madison, a non-Quaker, in 1794.

Philadelphia without her parents' interference, so they crossed the Delaware River to New Jersey.

The weather was cold. The wind blew hard. The river was a mile wide, and the current was strong. Yet their love was strong, too. In a small boat, they set sail that windy November evening. It was dark, for they had waited until after work to run away.

They sailed five miles downstream and crossed safely. Their destination was Hugg's Tavern on the waterfront in Gloucester, New Jersey. There the tavern owner, William Hugg, greeted them. William, a close friend of John's, had arranged for a justice of the peace to perform the ceremony.

Family tradition says the couple was married in front of the big fireplace of Hugg's Tavern. Beside them stood a tall grandfather clock with only an hour hand. The clock has since disappeared, but the fireplace still stands in Gloucester.

Betsy's parents apparently never forgave her for marrying outside her religion. The Quakers, however, gave Betsy two more chances to repent. Each time, she refused. Finally, on May 24, 1774, she was "read out of Meeting."

The record says, "Elizabeth Ross, late Griscom... having had her Education and made profession with us the People called Quakers...hath disunited herself from the Religious Fellowship with us."

Despite this difficulty, Betsy and John were happy. They joined Christ Church, a big change for

Christ Church stands on Second Street in Philadelphia. It was built between 1727 and 1744.

Betsy. Quaker Meetings were silent for they had no minister to lead a service. The services at Christ Church had singing and sermons.

For years Betsy worshipped at Christ Church. Today, her pew is marked with her name. A small American flag hangs by it.

John and Betsy struggled to make their dream of owning their own shop come true. They continued working at Webster's Upholstery Shop. Their apprenticeships were over, and now they were paid for their work. They saved enough money for John to buy upholstery tools and for Betsy to buy the needles, thread, and other things she needed.

These years were difficult for the young couple. Tensions ran high between the American colonies and England.

The tax problems between the colonies and England remained. Many of the taxes that the colonists hated had ended. But by 1773, King George III had made up his mind. He would show his bothersome colonists that he had the right to tax them whether they liked it or not.

The tax on tea sent to the colonies would be kept.

This tea tax helped unite the thirteen separate colonies as nothing else had. Before this time, each colony acted on its own.

Now the colonists resisted England together. They refused to buy tea. Instead, they brewed "Liberty tea" made from sassafras roots or other plants. While not as tasty as tea from India, Liberty tea sent a strong message to the British. The colonies showed they could stand together on an issue.

King George was just as stubborn. In 1773, a shipload of tea arrived in Boston. The colonists refused to let it be unloaded because they would not pay the tea tax. The angry colonists broke open the tea chests and dumped the tea into Boston Harbor. This event was called the Boston Tea Party.

Philadelphians read about the Boston Tea Party on December 24, 1773. Elizabeth Drinker wrote of reading, "An account from Boston, of 342 Chests of tea, being thrown into the Sea."

When the tea party news reached England, King George grew angry. How dare these upstart colonists disobey him! Ruining a whole cargo of valuable tea was too much.

He ordered that no ships could enter or leave Boston until every leaf of tea was paid for. To enforce his order, an army was sent to occupy Boston. Huge British warships blocked the harbor.

Meanwhile, Philadelphians faced a tea problem of

Bostonians gathered at Griffin's Wharf in Boston on December 16, 1773. There, 150 men and boys disguised as Native Americans dumped tea into Boston Harbor.

their own. The British ship *Polly* was heading for Philadelphia with a cargo of tea.

A pilot was needed to guide a ship up the winding Delaware River to Philadelphia. Colonists warned the pilots that "tar and feathers will be his portion" for anyone who guided the *Polly*.

Pilots refused to help the *Polly*. Who wanted to be covered with hot tar and have feathers poured over them?

Captain Ayres of the *Polly*, however, made up his mind to bring the tea to Philadelphia. He sailed until he reached Gloucester, New Jersey, the same place Betsy and John had been married only a year before.

On December 27, the State House bell in Philadelphia called folks to meet. More than 8,000 people, about a quarter of the city's population, answered the call. Knowing Betsy's and John's strong patriotic feelings, it is easy to imagine them in this cheering crowd.

The Philadelphians sent a strong message to Captain Ayres: Do not bring the tea into our city.

Seeing so many colonists united against him, Captain Ayres sailed away. The tea was not unloaded.

Other colonies had similar small victories. Tea was destroyed or returned in New York, New Jersey, Maryland, North Carolina, and South Carolina.

The storm of war was coming closer.

That same summer, men representing all thirteen colonies traveled to Philadelphia. They were to make plans to fight against the king. They would organize help for Boston. The representatives called themselves the Continental Congress. They met in Carpenters' Hall, one of the buildings Betsy's father had helped build.

In one stirring speech, Patrick Henry of Virginia declared, "I am not a Virginian. I am an American."

His words echoed the feelings of many colonists. If the thirteen colonies spoke with one voice, maybe they could persuade King George to change his mind.

In 1775, very few people wanted independence from Great Britain. Many colonists still felt they were British. But more and more felt that they were American first, British second. Betsy and John Ross felt this way, too.

Then, in April 1775, shocking news reached Philadelphia. British soldiers had fired upon and killed citizens of Massachusetts. These shots "heard round the world" were the first guns fired in the American Revolution.

The storm had finally broken. Philadelphia, in the center of the colonies, was chosen as the site for Congress to meet again. The Second Continental

Congress met in 1775. This time they came together in the State House and decided an American army was needed. George Washington was chosen to lead this army. His goal was to free the people of Boston from the British army.

Betsy and John probably joined the happy crowd gathered to wish Washington and his troops well. On June 21, 1775, the State House bell called thousands to gather to cheer Washington as his army marched to aid Boston.

One biographer of Washington described him: "He was now in the vigor of his days. Forty-three years old, stately, noble, and calm. As he sat his horse with grace, his military presence delighted every eye."

That same year, Betsy and John began their own revolution. They wanted the freedom of running their own business. They would finally open their own upholstery shop.

Betsy and John left Webster's shop. They moved to a small brick building on Arch Street. They lived upstairs. In the front room downstairs, they opened their upholstery shop. Outside they hung a sign, which read JOHN ROSS, UPHOLSTERER. History does not tell us why Betsy's name was not on the sign.

Starting a business on their own was daring. They were young and had no money from their parents. War was breaking out. But Betsy and John were skilled upholsterers and were determined to build a successful business.

This proved to be a more difficult task than they had imagined.

WAR

WITH A WAR THREATENING, THE city of Philadelphia bustled. The Continental Congress had brought many people to town. Soldiers marched down the streets to beating drums and piping fifes. Hardware stores sold all the swords, knapsacks, pistols, muskets, lead, and gunpowder they had. Shopkeepers wished they had more.

The first mention of stars for an American flag was this short poem in the *Massachusetts Spy* newspaper in 1774.

> *A ray of bright glory*
> *Now beams from afar;*

The American ensign [flag]
Now sparkles a star.

Great Britain's flag, the red, white, and blue Union Jack, still fluttered over America. The colonists might be preparing for war, but they had not yet declared independence.

Patriotic shipbuilders began building or changing ships to be privateers. These small ships had the permission of the Continental Congress to attack larger British merchant ships to get supplies America needed.

Britain in 1775 had the largest navy in the world. Its ships controlled the Atlantic Ocean. But the ocean is vast. The pesky privateers could capture a merchant ship and escape before a warship found them. Many privateers used Philadelphia as their port. Here they could sell the cloth, gunpowder, guns, and cannons the patriots needed.

The markets were busy, too. Farmers brought in their harvest of fruits, vegetables, cider, corn,

Delegates of the First Continental Congress leave Carpenters' Hall in Philadelphia.

wheat, and meats. Wagon loads of firewood were carted into town. Dried hides were traded. Sugar, fine woods, and fruit arrived from the West Indies. Iron, hardware, fabrics, and manufactured English items still trickled in.

Betsy and John spent long hours in their shop. They had no apprentices to help them. When a customer brought in a chair frame to be covered, John and Betsy went to work. Betsy displayed the fabrics she had on hand. Sometimes she took the customer's money to buy the fabric he wanted.

John used his tools to tightly stretch canvas straps on chair bottoms. He firmly fixed the canvas seat, then stuffed it with horsehair or moss. Goose feathers were very expensive and saved for the best customers. The stuffing was then sewn in to hold it in place. This might have been a job they shared or Betsy did alone.

Betsy cut the fabric for the chair and seamed it. John fit the fabric and tacked it into place with brass tacks. Before long, the beautiful and comfortable chair was finished.

Betsy also made tablecloths, bed curtains, drapes, and mattresses.

Betsy and John worked six days a week in their shop. They opened early and closed late. Sundays were a day of rest. They went to Christ Church, visited friends, took walks, and enjoyed each other's company.

John and Betsy were patriots. Although raised as a peace-loving Quaker, Betsy strongly supported the colonists' efforts against Britain.

Many Quakers refused to have anything to do with the patriots and their increasingly violent actions. Quakers were peaceful. They believed they should not fight in any wars.

Not every colonist in Philadelphia was a patriot. Many still supported King George and Parliament. They were called Tories. As the patriots became more vocal, Tories became quieter. They did not want the patriots' anger turned on them. They did not want to lose their possessions or have their homes attacked. They certainly did not want to be tarred and feathered.

Some families became divided, including John Ross's. One of his uncles, Colonel George Ross, was a patriot. He served in the Continental Congress and was active on committees raising money and supplies for General Washington's army. Another uncle named John Ross supported the king.

As a patriot, Betsy was as strong-minded as when she stood up against her parents and married John. Betsy joined a group called "The Fighting Quakers," who supported the war. Its members had all been "read out of Meeting."

Now Betsy and John would do everything they could to support the patriots' cause.

John recruited soldiers. He became a member of the local militia that marched, drilled, and prepared for battle. They waited for General Washington to call them into his army. While they waited, they guarded Philadelphia, protected the gunpowder, cannons, and muskets stored in town, and kept a watchful eye on the Tories.

Supplies for Washington's army became hard to get. British warships patrolled the American coast.

Privateers, instead of capturing ships, were being captured themselves. Still, a few brave captains managed to slip down the Delaware River, capture a British merchant ship, and bring the much-needed supplies back to Philadelphia.

One captain was Esek Hopkins, commodore of the new American navy. Congress created a navy of seven ships to capture supplies.

Hopkins was daring. In early December 1775, he set sail with his ships. Not finding any British ships to capture, he sailed to the Bahamas, a British island colony in the Atlantic.

He attacked New Providence, the capital, and captured the British fort guarding it. The Americans carried off gunpowder, cannonballs, muskets, and bullets. Best of all, they took 100 brass cannons. The fleet hastily returned to Philadelphia.

Washington desperately needed the captured supplies. His meager army surrounded Boston. They had few muskets, little gunpowder, and hardly any cannons.

As soon as the supplies were unloaded, they were

George Washington was an experienced leader. He had fought his first battle in 1754 during the French and Indian War.

taken to General Washington at Boston. Some materials, however, were left behind. It was winter and travel was difficult. These were stored in a warehouse until they could be safely moved. A guard was posted around them. Congress did not want Philadelphia Tories to steal them. John Ross was one of the guards.

January 1, 1776, Betsy's twenty-fourth birthday, arrived. That same day the new American flag was first raised near Boston. This flag was called the Continental Colors. General Washington wanted a new flag to fly for his new army on New Year's Day.

This flag had thirteen red and white stripes. A small Union Jack was in the canton, the top left-hand corner. The red and white stripes stood for the thirteen united colonies. The Union Jack remained to show the British that the colonies were loyal to the king.

During the fall of 1775 and winter of 1776, John practiced with the militia. He guarded the captured war supplies. Betsy ran the shop on her own. She took orders, made goods, and kept their business

The Continental Colors first flew in 1776.

records. Like many people, she hoped the colonies and England would patch up their differences. When they did, John could return to his work full-time. Business would be better because more fabrics, tacks, and goods would arrive from England.

One cold January day John proudly put on his uniform and marched off to guard the gunpowder. Later, Betsy heard a knock at her door. Expecting a customer, she quickly opened it to the chilly wind outside. A group of quiet militiamen stood in the street. Between them they carried a wounded man.

It was her husband, John Ross.

The men carried John's bloody, battered body upstairs to his bed. They told Betsy some gunpowder had exploded. John was caught by the blast.

Betsy took care of John. She cleaned his wounds, fed him broth, and nursed him. But his injuries were too great. Within days, John Ross died.

John was buried in the cemetery of Christ Church. He was the first church member to perish in the war. The records of Christ Church say, "John Ross, upholsterer, died January 21, 1776. Buried in C.C. [Christ Church Burial Ground]."

After the funeral, Betsy bravely walked home in the snow. She was alone in the world. Barely twenty-four years old, she was a widow.

What could she do? Return to her parents' home? No, she would have to give up the independence she and John had worked so hard for. Sell the upholstery shop? No, she and John had put their hearts and hands into the business.

Alone at home, Betsy Ross made a decision. She would keep the shop open and run it herself. Hadn't Aunt Sarah run her own business? If Aunt Sarah could do it, Betsy could, too.

UPHOLSTERER

ETSY COURAGEOUSLY FACED HER new life. Her parents invited her to return home. Betsy wanted to remain independent and continue to make her dream with John come true. The Ross Upholstery business would survive.

Betsy hung a tin sign in her window: ELIZABETH ROSS, UPHOLSTERER.

In the same window she placed samples of her craft: pillows decorated with her fine silk embroidery, a covered chair, fabrics, and cushions.

Someone looking in would see Betsy busy stitching.

Despite her hard work, Betsy fell on hard times. The war had slowed imports of fabrics, needles, and strong thread from England. She made do with cloth made in America, but it was of poorer quality.

Few people wanted to spend money on new furnishings, especially if war came to Philadelphia. To make ends meet, Betsy sewed clothes for soldiers.

The pace of life in Philadelphia, however, was busier than ever. Congress met at the State House. Delegates filled the coffee shops and taverns. Those in need of a new coat or shirt sometimes came to Betsy's small shop.

A Ross family story tells that George Washington turned to Betsy when he needed new shirts. Her grandson William Claypoole wrote, "While he was yet Colonel, Washington had visited her shop both professionally and socially many times."

John's uncle, Colonel George Ross, was a good friend of Washington's. Washington, George Ross, Betsy and John Ross had sometimes chatted after services at Christ Church.

All spring Betsy struggled. She grieved for John. But she was still determined to succeed. If only she could get some steady business, she could keep her independence.

General Washington was the man of the hour. His ragtag colonial army had forced the British out of Boston. Using the cannons John Ross had protected and others captured from the British, Washington surrounded Boston. One morning the surprised British soldiers saw many cannons aimed at them. They abandoned Boston and sailed away.

Everywhere General Washington went, crowds cheered him. With him in command, many patriots like Betsy felt King George would agree to the changes the colonists wanted.

Philadelphians whispered about the meetings of Congress. The meetings were secret, but word leaked out. Were all the colonies really thinking about declaring independence?

Sewing in her shop, Betsy must have thought about this, too. She struggled with her own independence. She must have wondered how the colonies would fare if they were independent, too. Would there be more war? Would the tear between England and its colonies ever be mended?

According to her family, one June day Betsy heard a knock on her door. She was surprised to see

Colonel George Ross. With him were two men: Robert Morris and General Washington.

Betsy invited them into her shop. She led them to her parlor. The parlor was the best room in the house. With such important men, Betsy could not conduct business in her shop.

There was a large fireplace lined with painted blue Dutch tiles. A tall mahogany cupboard with Betsy's best china stood in one corner. Close to the fireplace was her small dining table.

Settled in her parlor, Colonel Ross told Betsy they represented a special committee of Congress appointed to have a flag made. They asked her if she could make one.

As Betsy later told the story to her family, she replied, "I do not know, I will try." If the gentlemen had a pattern, she would follow it.

The gentlemen did. They desired a flag similar to the Continental Colors which had been raised at Boston on January 1, 1776. The new flag would have thirteen stripes, each representing one of the thirteen colonies. Instead of the small Union Jack

(British flag) in the canton, however, there would be a field of blue with thirteen white stars.

General Washington spread a drawing of the proposed flag on her table.

Betsy saw that the flag was too square. She suggested the flag be wider and longer so that it would wave better in the wind.

William Claypoole wrote this about his grandmother's description of Washington's visit: "The alteration and redrawing of the design, which was done then and there by General Washington, in pencil, in her back parlor."

Unfortunately, this drawing has never been found. Maybe, some argue, it never existed.

As the story was told, General Washington handed Betsy a pattern for the stars they wanted.

Betsy looked at the pattern and again made a suggestion. The stars were six-pointed. Claypoole wrote, "Mrs. Ross at once said that this was wrong: the stars should be five-pointed."

The men thought a five-pointed star would be more difficult to make than a six-pointed one.

The flag that Betsy sewed had thirteen stripes and thirteen five-pointed stars.

"Nothing easier," Betsy replied. She folded a piece of paper. With one quick snip of her scissors she made a star with five points.

The committee was pleased and agreed to the five-pointed star.

Robert Morris told Betsy to go to his shipping wharf nearby on the Delaware River. Mr. Morris was a wealthy Philadelphian and a devoted patriot.

He told her one of his clerks would give her materials to make the flag. The committee kept the new design. They gave it to William Barrett, a talented painter who lived near Betsy. He was to paint a copy. Unfortunately, this painting has never been found.

The flag committee apparently approached other seamstresses to make flags based on different designs. When the flags were finished, they would be presented to Congress. The delegates would make a final decision about which would be the flag of the United States.

In June 1776, independence had not been declared. Obviously, Washington and his committee realized it soon would be.

Unknown to Betsy, but known to us today, Thomas Jefferson had been asked to write a declaration of independence. As Betsy worked on her flag, Jefferson was writing a few blocks away. Quill pen in hand, he drafted the declaration. When finished, this document would announce to the world that the thirteen British colonies in America were now the thirteen United States of America.

Betsy went to Mr. Morris's wharf. A clerk pulled an old flag out of a chest and gave it to her for a model. She would study the stitches peculiar to a ship's flag. She would hold the flag to test its bias. This way Betsy would know how to make a flag that would flutter in the wind.

What if my flag is chosen? she may have wondered. There would be flags to make for the American navy ships. Merchant ships would want the new flag, too. So might the army.

If her flag was accepted and she made many new flags, Betsy could keep her hard-won independence. Maybe she could even hire other seamstresses to help.

It is not hard to imagine Betsy Ross in her shop. She began by cutting a blue rectangle. Rocking in her chair by the parlor fireplace, she carefully cut out and stitched the thirteen five-pointed white stars onto it.

Taking a large piece of white material, she cut six long strips. From red material she cut seven strips. It was awkward. The material was thick. But her skilled hands and sharp scissors managed to cut the strips long and somewhat even.

Betsy Ross sews a flag at her home on Arch Street.

Betsy stitched late into the night. Outside, the summer sounds of the city quieted. Finally, the flag was finished.

One can imagine her standing, holding the flag, and hoping Congress would choose it.

As her grandson wrote, "The flag was soon finished, and Betsy returned it, the first 'Star Spangled Banner' that ever floated up on the breeze, to her employer."

With the committee watching, Betsy's flag was run up to the top of a ship's mast. Both she and the flag "received the unanimous approval of the committee." Onlookers agreed. They liked this new American flag.

Betsy's flag was taken to the State House. It, along with the other sample flags, was presented to Congress, with a report from the flag committee.

In her shop Betsy anxiously waited to hear if her flag had been chosen. What if they did not choose her flag? Then she would just have to find other work.

As Betsy apparently told her family, the next day

Colonel Ross came to her shop. He had good news. Her flag had been chosen!

He asked her to turn her attention to making flags. Sailors needed them. He would take as many as she could make. He told her to go out and buy all the supplies she needed. And be fast!

Betsy was overwhelmed. Since John had died, she had had only two big orders. These had been to furnish rooms with beds, carpets, and drapes. Now she had an order for all the flags she could make!

Her joy suddenly soured. How could she make hundreds of flags quickly? Being almost penniless, how she could buy the materials she needed?

Just as she made important decisions before, she would make this one, too. Hadn't she stood firm against her parents and married her beloved John Ross? Hadn't she stood firm and kept their shop open after John died?

Somehow she would find a way to buy the materials. She would also find a way to make hundreds of flags more easily than the first one.

FLAGS

BUT WHERE WAS SHE GOING TO GET money to buy the necessary materials? Betsy would need yards of sturdy material for the cantons and stripes, strong needles, and dozens of spools of heavy thread.

She had little money, but decided to buy what materials she could afford. She would make as many flags as possible. The committee would probably turn to other seamstresses to make the rest of the flags. Betsy could only do her best and be satisfied with it.

She began working on her next flag when someone knocked. Was it another customer?

It was Colonel Ross. According to William Canby, the colonel said, "It was very thoughtless of me that I did not offer to supply you with the means for making these purchases. Here is something to begin with."

Colonel Ross handed her some money to get her started. He told Betsy to draw on his credit for other supplies. Now Betsy Ross could go into the flag-making business.

While Betsy was making her flags, Congress was making its break with England. Unknown outside the State House, Thomas Jefferson's draft of the Declaration of Independence had been completed. On July 1, independence was debated by Congress.

When the debate ended, a vote was taken. Not all the delegates were there, however.

The next day they were. On July 2, another vote was made. All the colonies agreed.

John Adams of Massachusetts wrote to his wife, Abigail, "A resolution was passed without one dissenting Colony, 'that these United Colonies are, and of right ought to be, free and independent States.'"

Independence was declared!

Congress unanimously approved the Declaration of Independence on July 4. The document was sent to a printer. When it was ready, the declaration would be made public.

On July 8, 1776, the State House bell rang out. Thousands gathered in the yard behind the building. They wondered what news they would learn. Were the whispers about independence true?

Maybe Betsy Ross was in the crowd that sunny afternoon.

Christopher Marshall, a member of Congress, wrote, "[We] went in a body to the State House Yard, where in the presence of a great concourse [group] of people, the Declaration of Independence was read by John Nixon."

Colonel Nixon held up his hand to silence the crowd. He began reading. Loud cheers interrupted him as he read. At last he reached the end.

"Huzzah! Huzzah! Huzzah!" shouted the excited crowd. Drums rattled and guns were fired into the air. Bells tolled throughout Philadelphia. Bands played and people paraded. Fireworks burst overhead.

The Declaration of Independence was signed by all fifty-six members of the Second Continental Congress.

Marshall wrote, "There were bonfires, ringing bells, and other demonstrations of joy upon the unanimity and agreement of the Declaration."

Riders carried copies of the Declaration north and south, spreading the exciting news to the other colonies, now states.

On July 9, the Declaration was read in New York

to Washington's troops. They shouted and threw their hats into the air. A huge leaden statue of King George III was pulled down. Later, it was melted and molded into 42,000 bullets for the American army.

Abigail Adams described how Massachusetts received the news of independence: "Bells rang... cannons were discharged...every face appeared joyful."

She wrote, "Thus ends royal authority in this State. And all the people say Amen."

The king's coat of arms was torn down from the State House in Boston and every picture of him was burned.

Now the states, like Betsy, were on their own. Would they fight as hard as she did to survive?

MARRIED AGAIN

EXCITEMENT FOR INDEPENDENCE RAN high for the patriots throughout the former colonies. But the patriots struggled early in the war.

On August 27, 1776, more than 22,000 British soldiers and Hessians (hired German soldiers) defeated Washington's army of 10,000 men. Long Island and New York were captured.

The British turned to Philadelphia, the American capital and soul of the revolution. They hoped to conquer the rebel capital by Christmas and quickly end the war.

Washington retreated from New York to New Jersey. The British army followed. Washington crossed the Delaware River to Pennsylvania. The

British troops landed in Alpine, New Jersey, on November 20, 1776.
They were pursuing General Washington's army.

British continued across New Jersey. Philadelphia was their goal.

Only about 400 militiamen protected Philadelphia. Betsy and thousands of patriots wondered if the British would capture their city.

Wisely, Washington ordered all boats along the New Jersey side of the river to be brought to the opposite shore in Pennsylvania. Without transportation, the British would be stuck in New Jersey.

General Howe could not cross the river without the missing boats. He would have to wait until the river froze to capture Philadelphia.

Congress, fearful of capture itself, moved the government to Baltimore. There they hoped to be safe.

Most Philadelphians, like the widow Betsy Ross, had no choice. They had to stay in Philadelphia and carry on with their lives. Betsy's upholstering business came to a standstill. Fortunately, she had flags to make.

Some of Betsy's customers included local sea captains. Many were merchants trying to slip past British ships on the Delaware Bay. Others were privateers, captains given permission by Congress to capture British ships and supplies.

One of these captains was Joseph Ashburn. Betsy had known Joseph since childhood. He had enjoyed blue-eyed Betsy's spark and spunk. He had wanted to marry her, but she had chosen John Ross instead.

Joseph Ashburn had grown up boating on the Delaware. He went to sea at an early age. When he was twenty-one, his aunt placed him in command of a ship she owned called the *Swallow*. In the *Swallow*, Captain Ashburn voyaged to the West Indies to bring supplies back to Philadelphia.

This was dangerous work. British ships prowled the Atlantic Ocean. They wanted to capture every rebel ship they could.

A sad fate awaited those who were captured. They were usually jailed in horrible British prisons, where hundreds grew sick and died.

North of Philadelphia, General Washington worried. Many of his soldiers would be leaving on December 31, when their duty time ended. He had lost New York. It looked like he would soon lose Philadelphia, as well.

Discouraged, Washington wrote to a friend on December 18, 1776, "I think the game is pretty near up." The young United States looked like it would not last until the new year of 1777 began.

Washington had to do something. Up to this point he had retreated before the advancing British. What if he attacked? The British would not expect such bold action from him. Knowing the Hessian soldiers would be celebrating Christmas, Washington planned to cross the Delaware River. He would surprise the Hessians with a dawn attack on December 26.

The moon was almost full on December 25. There was enough light for the dangerous crossing.

An American officer wrote, "It is fearfully cold and raw and a snow storm is setting in. It will be a terrible night for the men who have no shoes. Some of them have tied old rags around their feet, others are barefoot."

The American army began crossing the Delaware. They rowed the boats Washington had kept from the British. Great chunks of ice smacked into the tiny fleet. All night long, men, horses, cannons, and supplies were ferried to the New Jersey shore.

Then it began to rain and sleet. Undaunted, the Americans marched the nine miles to Trenton, New Jersey.

At daybreak they attacked the unsuspecting Hessians.

The Hessians, many of them asleep, were totally unprepared for Washington's attack. The Americans

General Washington and his troops crossed the icy Delaware River during their advance to Trenton, New Jersey, on December 25, 1776. This dramatic painting shows an American flag onboard Washington's boat.

captured more than 1,000 Hessian soldiers and their equipment.

The Hessian supplies were much needed by the Americans. With the captured food, warm clothes, guns, and powder, maybe Washington's men could make it through the winter.

Lord George Germain, King George's Secretary for the Colonies, later said in Parliament, "All our hopes were blasted by that unhappy affair at Trenton."

The next week, Washington led his troops into battle against the British army at Princeton. The British, under the command of Lord Cornwallis, were driven from the battlefield.

In two weeks, the American army had won two battles!

After the victories at Trenton and Princeton, Philadelphia was saved. The tables, however, would turn the next year.

Betsy Ross scraped by. Firewood and food grew scarce. Always a hard worker, Betsy kept cutting and sewing flags.

When the Delaware River froze completely, Captain Joseph Ashburn could not voyage to the West Indies.

In the spring Betsy was paid for her flags. This is the only written document about her flag-making business. It reads, "State Navy Board, May 1777. An order on William Webb to Elizabeth Ross, for fourteen pounds, twelve shillings, two pence for making ships' colors [flags]."

That winter and spring the friendship between

Captain Joseph Ashburn and Betsy Ross grew. Even though he already had flags for his ship, Captain Ashburn frequently visited the Widow Ross. When he asked Betsy to marry him, she agreed.

On June 15, 1777, Betsy and Joseph were married at Old Swede's Church in Philadelphia. Betsy was now Elizabeth Ross Ashburn.

The Ashburns lived at Betsy's home on Arch Street.

Just the day before Betsy and Joseph were married, June 14, 1777, Congress passed this resolution.

"Resolved—That the Flag of the united states be 13 stripes alternate red and white, that the Union be 13 stars white in a blue field representing a new constellation."

Betsy's flag, by this resolution, was now the official flag of the United States of America.

June 14 is celebrated across America as Flag Day.

MORE FLAGS

ETSY WAS SOON BUSIER THAN EVER before. Now that the colors had been firmly established, the navy wanted more flags.

Not all American flags looked the same. The red and white stripes were standard. But Congress did not say in which pattern the stars should be. They said the United States was a "new constellation."

Captain Ashburn sailed with a flag made by Betsy. They agreed early in their marriage that she would continue with her shop. He would continue sailing.

July 8, 1777, was a day of celebration in Philadelphia. The United States was a year old! Bells rang. Bands played. Crowds cheered.

The Pennsylvania Packet newspaper said, "Around noon, all the armed ships and galleys in the river were drawn up before the city, [dressed] in the gayest manner with the colors of the United States." Most likely, dozens of Betsy's flags fluttered from the masts.

Early in August, British General Howe set off again for Philadelphia. This time he had 228 ships and 19,000 men. Some of his army would sail up the Delaware to capture Philadelphia. The rest would march across New Jersey again and attack by land.

Washington knew his small army would be no match for General Howe. To put on a brave show, he marched his 11,000 men through Philadelphia. They sang the popular "Yankee Doodle" as they marched. Washington rode in the lead.

Betsy most likely put down her scissors to watch the very first parade of the Continental army.

When the army left to fight the British, the city went into a panic. More patriots left. Heavy carts rumbled over the cobblestone streets day and night. Other Philadelphians dug secret holes to bury jewels, gold, and valuables.

The Liberty Bell was taken out of Philadelphia in September 1777. It would not be hung in the State House steeple again until 1785.

Bells were taken down. The bells, if captured, could be melted and their brass forged into British cannons. The great State House bell, which had rung for the Declaration of Independence, was removed. It was loaded onto a cart and taken out of Philadelphia. The Liberty Bell was hidden in a church in Allentown, Pennsylvania.

Joseph Ashburn was home from the sea. His knowledge of ships was greatly needed. The

Pennsylvania navy was given the task of preventing Howe's ships from reaching Philadelphia.

Small ships were built and armed with cannons. Gunpowder was so scarce that a few ships carried men with bows and arrows.

Betsy's flags flew at the peak of many of these vessels.

On September 11, cannons were heard booming at Brandywine, twenty-five miles from Philadelphia. Betsy waited for news of the battle.

Riders galloped into the city that evening. The news was bad. Washington had lost!

Washington desperately called for more men. John Claypoole answered his call. He was a friend of Betsy's from childhood.

He joined the Continental army on September 13, 1777. The war files record for that date states, "John Claypoole was commissioned a Second Lieutenant in Colonel Jehu Eyre's regiment."

The war had taken a grim turn for the Americans. Their puny navy was no match for the British ships. On land Lord Cornwallis marched steadily toward Philadelphia.

The weather was hot and humid on the morning of September 26, 1777. Farmers, fleeing Cornwallis, galloped into the city. They shouted that the British were at Germantown, six miles away. Shopkeepers closed their doors. Teachers sent their students home. Bakers put out their fires.

In 1778, Great Britain's Lord Charles Cornwallis (above) became second in command to Sir Henry Clinton.

Families fled without even taking their belongings. They swamped the rowboats and ferries crossing the Delaware to New Jersey.

In the distance came the sounds of the British drums and fifers. The rumble of the British cannons and marching men sounded like faraway thunder. The noise grew louder as the British entered Philadelphia.

They marched down Germantown Road, turned

onto Second Street, crossing Arch Street near
Betsy's home.

Those patriots still in town stood on the sidewalks
and street corners. One patriot wrote, "Cornwallis
came with a brilliant staff and escort...followed by
long trains of artillery and squadrons of light
dragoons [soldiers on horseback], the best in the
army." The drummers and fifers played as the
patriots watched helplessly.

The British army seemed endless. Cornwallis
stopped at the abandoned State House. His officers
made the halls of Congress their home. Soldiers
camped in the State House yard where the
Declaration of Independence had been read.

Tories flocked to the British. They guided them to
the best patriot houses. Lord Cornwallis took over a
rich merchant's home. Captain Andre moved into
Benjamin Franklin's home. The Penn mansion was
saved for General Howe.

Other officers and soldiers took over the homes of
patriots. If the home had been abandoned, that was
fine. If the home was occupied by a patriot, they were

told to leave. Betsy's home was looked at, but it was so small that the British did not bother taking it.

A cavalry troop camped in Carpenters' Hall, which Betsy's father had helped build. The British used the weather vane on top for target practice.

Knowing that Washington would not attack now, the British settled in for the winter in Philadelphia. Patriots, like Betsy, wondered about their future. She was a known rebel, a firm patriot, and made American flags. Some British soldiers nicknamed her "Little Rebel."

Betsy did not have to wait long to find out what was in store.

CHAPTER 11

THE LONG WINTER

LORD CORNWALLIS TOOK CONTROL OF Philadelphia. He rode the streets making sure his men did no great harm to the city. He put an end to horse racing on city streets. He inspected his troops. He directed the building of defenses. Lord Cornwallis would have Philadelphia firmly in his grasp when General Howe reached the city.

Betsy did not stop making flags. She kept her shop open downstairs along the street. Most likely, she sewed flags upstairs at night in her bedroom.

The British counted 5,470 houses. Owners of 587 of them had fled, leaving the homes empty. Open for business were 287 stores. Not counting the enemy soldiers, 21,767 people lived in Philadelphia.

Betsy did not see Joseph very often. The American ships hugged the New Jersey shore. If the British ships came, the rebels would escape upstream.

The Americans heard General Howe had landed and was marching to Philadelphia. Betsy, like other patriots, hoped Washington would attack.

Washington did. On the foggy morning of October 3, Washington's troops opened fire on the British at Germantown. Betsy could hear the rumble of the cannons six miles away. Lord Cornwallis was alerted and galloped to the battle.

With the fog as a cover, Washington's men surprised the British. They drove them back into Germantown. The British made a stand in a stone house. Many American soldiers died.

Then General Howe attacked. John Claypoole, Betsy's friend, fought bravely in hand-to-hand combat. A cannonball exploded near him. He fell to the ground with a sharp pain in his side. The Americans were driving the British back.

The fog then played a cruel trick on the Americans. It had helped in the attack until two groups of Americans became confused in the fog. They started shooting at each other, not the enemy.

The other Americans began retreating, then running. John's friends carried him to safety. Sadly, the battle was lost to the British.

General Howe marched into Philadelphia. He ordered that the State House serve as a hospital for wounded British and American soldiers. Soon the halls overflowed with men who earlier that day had been shooting at one another.

Betsy and many other women turned their skilled hands to making bandages. They carried food to wounded men. They took care of friend and foe alike.

Many injured British were put in Philadelphia's few hospitals. Captured Americans, if not in the State House, were put in the nearby Walnut Street prison. Conditions there were horrible.

The British soldier in charge of the prison would not let Betsy and others help the rebels. Food ran out, wounds became infected, and disease spread among the Americans. Many died and were buried in pits in a field across the street. Today this field, Washington Square Park, holds an untold number of unmarked graves of American soldiers.

Washington and his men retreated to Valley Forge where they would spend a winter of hardship. He did, however, post patrols around Philadelphia to keep Howe trapped in the city until spring. This made it difficult for supplies to reach the city.

One writer said, "Nothing scarcely, which is used by people of every Rank can be very long cheap here." He was right.

Every day food became harder to get. Flour, butter, and eggs were rarely seen in the markets anymore. Beef and pork were scarce. Prices rapidly rose. Even if food could be found, it was often too expensive to buy.

"Such is the distressed situation we are in," complained a housewife. But the many patriots in Philadelphia were determined to carry on, no matter how difficult things became.

General Washington speaks with the Marquis de Lafayette at Valley Forge during the terrible winter of 1777–1778. Lafayette, who came from France, served as a major general under Washington.

Firewood soon ran out. The British burned the Philadelphians' furniture for cooking and heating.

Betsy found it hard to get the supplies she needed. Patriots at two small forts, Fort Mercer and Fort Mifflin, kept British ships from reaching the city. A few things trickled in from the active privateers.

All this time Betsy did not know where her husband, Joseph, was. Was he in the fighting at Fort Mercer? Had he taken a ship and escaped?

General Howe was furious about the lack of supplies. He ordered Lord Cornwallis to destroy Fort Mercer and Fort Mifflin. Turning the full force of his men against the forts, they finally fell, but not without a struggle.

Betsy learned Joseph had escaped with his ship upstream. He would spend the winter there. She would find a way to survive the winter in Philadelphia.

With a steady supply of goods, the British army settled in for a winter of ease in Philadelphia. There were parties and plays, dinners and dances. Even with the high prices, the British could afford many luxuries.

Betsy turned her efforts away from flags that winter. Her sewing skills were needed. Like other brave patriotic women, she made coats, shirts, blankets, socks, and pants in secret. She gathered shoes and boots. She mixed medicines. These were smuggled out of Philadelphia to Washington's desperate troops. One family story tells that Betsy even made cartridges for American muskets.

General Howe knew Washington's army was

camped at Valley Forge, fewer than twenty miles away. Howe was too comfortable to leave Philadelphia. He felt he could wait until spring to attack Washington. Then he would end this annoying war and go home to England.

This came sooner than Howe expected. King George was angry that war continued. Howe was ordered back to England. The king also ordered that Philadelphia be abandoned. The British were to make New York their headquarters again.

A huge party was given for the departing British. Hundreds of finely dressed Tories ate and danced at this celebration, which lasted all afternoon and night. Patriotic seamstresses like Betsy Ross Ashburn refused to make dresses for the event.

Silently, the patriots were celebrating. The hated British were leaving their beloved city.

On June 18, 1778, the British army marched out, and their ships sailed away.

The rebels held a celebration of their own. It was like a second declaration of independence.

American flags, hidden from the British, flew once again. Congress returned.

Happily for Betsy, Joseph Ashburn sailed his *Swallow* to the wharf at the end of Race Street. Joseph was safely home!

Life began to return to normal for the Ashburns. The war still continued but had moved away from Philadelphia. Betsy made flags again and sewed clothes for the American army. Joseph began making his privateering voyages again. Whenever he returned, he brought Betsy fabrics and materials. The Ashburns weren't rich, but they were comfortable.

On September 15, 1779, the Ashburns welcomed their first daughter into the world. They called her Zilla.

As the war continued, Betsy still made the sturdy flags.

Then one day, Betsy hugged Joseph good-bye. He was sailing on a voyage to the West Indies. They didn't know that this would be the last time they would ever see each other.

ALONE AGAIN

JOSEPH ASHBURN WAS A SKILLED SEA captain. But his ship, the *Swallow*, was old. Captain Ashburn was offered command of a new ship being built in Philadelphia. After talking with Betsy, they agreed he should take this opportunity.

The new ship wouldn't be finished until spring. Captain Ashburn was eager to return to sea. He joined another new ship, the *Patty*. He would serve as first mate until his ship was ready.

The *Patty* was bigger than the *Swallow*. She carried nineteen crew members and six new brass cannons. She would sail to the West Indies. If any British merchant ships crossed her path, she would capture them as prizes.

Many privateers departed from the port of Philadelphia on the Delaware River in 1780.

Betsy walked with Joseph to the *Patty*. He carried "Betsy's flag," as he always called it. This flag had flown on his *Swallow*. Now it would fly on the *Patty*.

Waving from shore, Betsy said good-bye to her husband. Early in October 1780, the *Patty* sailed downstream and was soon out of sight.

At the same time John Claypoole was also going

to sea. His old wounds had been hurting him, and he had left the army. For a while he had worked in his family's tanning trade, but he grew bored. After all of the action of war, tanning leather did not suit him.

John grew restless. Like Joseph Ashburn, he joined a privateer. He set sail on November 7, 1780, aboard the *Luzerne*. This ship was bound for France to get supplies. To keep track of his days, John Claypoole kept a journal. It was small enough to fit into his coat pocket.

Most of Joseph Ashburn's trips to the Indies lasted six weeks. Since the *Patty* was newer and faster, Betsy hoped he would return home sooner. After all, their second child would be born in February. She wanted Joseph home by then.

Five weeks passed, but she did not worry. Then six weeks, seven weeks, eight weeks went by without any word. Betsy wondered and worried.

Every day Betsy walked to the State House to read the news posted there. Nothing about the *Patty*. She went to the offices of the men who owned the ship.

No news was found there, either. She asked each captain returning to Philadelphia if he had heard anything. "No" was the repeated answer.

January 1, 1781, came. It was Betsy's twenty-ninth birthday.

On February 25, 1781, baby Eliza was born. Holding her second daughter, Betsy wondered if the lively Eliza would ever meet her father. On her own, Betsy took care of Zilla and Eliza, ran her business, and worried about Joseph.

Winter turned to spring—still no word about Joseph and the *Patty*. John Claypoole aboard the *Luzerne* had safely crossed the Atlantic and reached France. He got sick and spent weeks in bed. When he recovered, the heavily loaded *Luzerne* set sail for home. The French cannons, gunpowder, guns, and cloth were much needed by the American troops.

The winds blew fair, and the *Luzerne* made good passage. The crew were excited. Soon they would be home with family and friends. Then disaster struck.

John described it this way in his journal:

On the fourth of April as we were pleasantly sailing and pleasing ourselves with the prospect of soon being home, all hands in high spirits. Fortune, that fickle jade, threw a Privateer [English] in our way who soon made prize of us and with us shaped her course for Ireland.

John Claypoole was a British prisoner of war.

He wrote, "Thirty-seven in number were sent under guard and in irons to the town of Limerick [Ireland]." There they were imprisoned. A few weeks later he was forced to march seventy-two miles to the seaport, Cork. The Americans were placed on the British prison ship *Lenox*.

The British tried to get the Americans to join them. They offered them their freedom. John and many other patriots refused. Better to die a prisoner than turn traitor to their country!

In June the *Lenox* sailed from Ireland to England. The Americans would join their fellows in the Old Mill Prison at Plymouth. This was the worst prison in all of England.

On September 1, 1781, John wrote this in his journal: "We have been now about two months [in prison] and for aught I know shall be here two years, for I do not see any likely hood of our being exchanged."

Sometimes during the long war, captured British officers were exchanged for captured American officers. John did not think this would happen to him.

There were more than 300 American prisoners in Old Mill Prison. They had no medical care. Food and water were scarce. Forty days in "the black hole" was punishment for trying to escape. John wrote, "Notwithstanding we very often attempt to make our escape but there is so strict a guard kept over us that very few effect [make] it."

Every day more prisoners arrived. One day John Claypoole watched a new group of captured Americans shuffle through the prison gate. A bearded man caught his attention.

It was his friend Joseph Ashburn! The *Patty* had been captured almost a year earlier. Ashburn had been on a prison ship for months. Even with the threat of hanging, Ashburn and Claypoole refused to betray their country.

At home in Philadelphia, Betsy had no clue as to her husband's whereabouts. She did not know if he was alive or not.

John Claypoole, despite the horrid conditions at the prison, remained healthy. Joseph Ashburn, however, grew weak. The damp weather, the poor food, and the lack of warm clothes took their toll. The young captain, so strong when he sailed from home, was now a weakened man.

News of the war trickled into the prison. The American army, weak, still fought on. Washington would not give up.

On November 25, 1781, a newspaper was smuggled into Old Mill Prison inside a loaf of bread. Loud cheers erupted from the Americans. Five weeks earlier Lord Cornwallis had surrendered his army to Washington at Yorktown. The war was as good as over.

The Americans celebrated. They cheered and

As Betsy waited for news about the fate of her husband, she carried on with her work at her Arch Street home.

paraded. They painted American flags on paper. They stuck the flags in their hats and marched around the prison yard. They shouted at their guards to open fire on them.

"Huzzah! Huzzah! Huzzah!" the rebels shouted.

Joseph and John hoped for a speedy exchange now that the war seemed over. Unfortunately, Joseph Ashburn's health grew worse. John nursed his friend the best he could.

In his diary John wrote this note: "In the night of the 3rd of March [1782] Mr. Joseph Ashburn departed this life after an illness of about a week."

Unknown to Betsy Ross Ashburn, her husband was buried in an unmarked grave in England.

Now that the war was almost over, the British began exchanging prisoners. On June 22, 1782, John Claypoole and 215 other rebel captives sailed for home.

Claypoole was excited to finally be free. But he faced one of the most challenging tasks of his life. Since Joseph had died in his arms, he wanted to be the one to tell Betsy of his death.

Fifty days later he reached Philadelphia. First, he would see his own family. Then, he would visit Betsy Ross Ashburn.

MRS. CLAYPOOLE

JOHN CLAYPOOLE RAN HOME. HE HUGGED his mother and sisters. They were pleased to see him. They had had no idea what had happened to him. Begging their pardon, he walked slowly to Betsy's home. Hat in hand, he knocked on her door.

Betsy greeted him and invited John back to her parlor. Baby Eliza rocked in her cradle. She had never seen her father. Three-year-old Zilla played in the garden.

Betsy had waited twenty months for word about her husband. She dreaded what John Claypoole was about to say.

John told about his capture and imprisonment. He talked about Joseph Ashburn's coming to Old

Mill Prison and their struggle to survive. Then he told Betsy of Joseph's sickness and death.

Betsy thanked him as he left. He thanked her for helping his sisters and mother while he was gone.

Quietly, Betsy closed her door. She was a widow once more.

How would she raise two children alone? Would she be able to keep her shop open? As hard as it was, her loss was no greater than that suffered by other patriot families. Many had lost husbands, brothers, and fathers in the war.

Betsy had carried on when Joseph was away. Now that he would never return, she would still carry on. She could make flags. She could sew clothes. She would run her shop as usual and do the best she could. She had no other choice.

John Claypoole rested and got stronger. He visited family and friends. He walked and talked with folks. More and more often his footsteps led him to Betsy's door.

Betsy welcomed him. They chatted while she worked. When she asked, he told her more of

Joseph's last days. She told him what had happened in America while he was in prison. She told him how Philadelphia celebrated when Cornwallis surrendered. She told him how she was determined to keep her upholstery shop open to support herself, Zilla, and Eliza.

John told Betsy about his future plans, too. He could not become a tanner now. His family's tannery had gone out of business during the war. He would rest and then look for work. His days as a soldier had ended.

The war, however, was not over. Minor battles were fought. The British navy still controlled the seas. In France the Americans and the British were working on a peace treaty to end the war formally.

In Paris, France, Ben Franklin (right) and British representative, Richard Oswald, discuss a peace treaty to end the American Revolution.

John Claypoole had liked life at sea. After two idle months at home, he decided to go to sea again. This time he sailed to the West Indies aboard the ship *Hyder Ally*. The skillful captain avoided capture, and John made several voyages.

Betsy missed John's visits. She missed him, too, just as he missed her. The time at sea made John realize that he was in love with Betsy.

After his last voyage, John asked Betsy to marry him. She agreed. On May 8, 1783, in Christ Church Betsy became Elizabeth Griscom Ross Ashburn Claypoole. And so she remained the rest of her life.

Betsy asked John to join her in her upholstery business. John was happy to agree. Betsy taught him how to upholster chairs and how to run a business. She also taught him how to make flags.

John brought many skills to the business, too. Having once worked in his family's tanning business, he knew how to do leather work. He began upholstering chairs in leather. From his experience in the army, he suggested that their shop make items for the army. The business grew as the Claypooles made army tents, canvas knapsacks, cots, beds, and chairs. They also repaired tents and other items.

Remembering his days as a sailor, John and Betsy began making things for ships. They made mattresses as well as furniture for ships.

For several years they continued to live in the small brick house on Arch Street. As the business grew, they needed more room. They also needed extra room for their family. On April 3, 1785, baby Clarissa was born. She was Betsy's third daughter. Then on November 15, 1786, another daughter, Susan, was born.

The Claypooles moved to a bigger home on Second Street. This was a house that Betsy's great-grandfather, Andrew Griscom, had built. Their move came at a sad time, however. Zilla, Betsy's oldest daughter, had died.

At the house on Second Street, John and Betsy's daughters Rachel and Jane were born. Betsy and John continued making flags and kept up the upholstery business. John even advertised the move to the new house.

"Claypoole, John, Upholsterer, Respectfully informs the Public . . . [that] he continues to carry on the business of Upholsterer in all its various branches . . ."

John had the good luck to get business from the state of Pennsylvania. The state needed new furniture, upholstered chairs, leather-covered desks, and various repairs. Together John and Betsy turned their energies to completing these jobs and raising their growing family.

When Betsy and John were first married, they worshipped at Christ Church. John's family had once been Quakers. Betsy still felt good about her Quaker childhood. The regular Quakers who were against war would not have Betsy and others back. So Betsy helped found the Free Quakers. These 400 Quakers had supported the war in various ways as Betsy had done. Together the Claypoole family worshipped at the Society of Free Quakers.

By 1783, the Free Quakers built their own house of worship. General Washington and Ben Franklin gave money to help with the building.

The American Revolution finally ended in 1783 when the United States and England signed the Treaty of Paris. America was free, but now she had to create a new government. It would be five years until the Constitution was signed.

The Constitution called for the election of a president. George Washington was elected unanimously to be the first president of the United States of America.

New York first served as the capital of the new nation. Then in 1790, Congress and the new president moved the capital to Philadelphia.

Betsy's business flourished as Philadelphia once again became the most important city in America. Chairs and sofas needed upholstering. Rooms needed drapes and carpets. Beds needed mattresses, curtains, and blankets.

And everyone seemed to want an American flag.

In 1793, yellow fever swept through Philadelphia. More than 20,000 people left the city to avoid becoming sick. Even George Washington moved to Germantown until frost stopped the spread of the yellow fever. Betsy's husband and children were spared. Her parents, however, both died from the deadly disease.

By early 1795, the Claypoole home was crowded again. There were five daughters and the business. Betsy's fourteen-year-old niece, Sarah, moved in, too. Betsy put everyone who was old enough to work in the shop. Just as she had learned a trade working in John Webster's Upholstery Shop, so Betsy's daughters and niece would learn a trade as well.

The Claypooles needed more room, so they moved again. They did not buy a home but rented one on Front Street. Here on December 20, 1795, Betsy's seventh daughter, Harriet, was born. Betsy had to suffer another heartbreak. Nine short months later, Harriet died. Despite their sadness, Betsy and John ran their shop and raised the other girls.

Betsy, as warmhearted as ever, even took in her sister Sarah's oldest daughter, Margaret. Margaret's husband and son had recently died. Alone, Margaret turned to Aunt Betsy for comfort. Betsy found room for her in her home and shop.

On May 1, 1795, the United States of America adopted this flag. It had fifteen stars and fifteen stripes. There was a star and stripe for each state, including the new states of Vermont and Kentucky.

Betsy had always cared for others before herself. Now she became the focus of the family. Nephews, nieces, and cousins turned to Betsy for advice or comfort. Betsy never failed to help them out.

With so many helpful hands in the shop, John Claypoole grew restless once more. He had served in the army. He had had many adventures at sea. Now he wanted to do other things with his many talents.

John was offered a job in the United States

Custom House dealing with ship cargoes. With Betsy's blessing he took the job. Now the large family had the extra money his job paid. But Betsy would not give up her shop. She had worked too long and hard to make it a success.

Over the years John's war wounds began to bother him. The hunger and sickness in prison had also hurt his health. In the early 1800s, his health grew worse. Finally, it was so bad that he had to quit his job. Betsy kept her shop open, even though she had to take care of him.

John's sickness grew so bad that he was forced to spend much of his time in bed. Betsy cared for him. She cheered him up when he felt sad. She told him stories about the work in the shop. Even while caring for John, Betsy was busy as usual. Her growing daughters were getting married. There were grandchildren to love and enjoy.

In 1812, the United States went to war with Britain again. During the War of 1812, Betsy's flag-making business boomed. There was a tremendous need for her flags. John and Betsy's oldest daughter,

Clarissa, and their niece, Margaret, helped make flags. They sold flags to merchants, ship owners, the army, and the navy.

John Claypoole never fully recovered his health. On August 13, 1817, he died. Betsy was sixty-five years old.

Betsy continued in business. Her family urged her to retire. Her hands were not as strong. Her eyesight was going bad. But Betsy enjoyed working. She ran her business for another ten years after John died.

Almost blind, Betsy could no longer cut the fabric or make her firm stitches. Still keen of mind and quick-witted, she retired. In 1827, when she was seventy-five, Betsy put her business in the capable hands of Clarissa and Margaret.

For years afterward she was still listed in the Philadelphia City Directory as "Elizabeth Claypoole, upholsterer."

When Betsy retired, she moved twelve miles to Abington, Pennsylvania. There she lived with her daughter Susan Claypoole Satterthwaite. Betsy's eyes may have given out, but not her energy. At

Susan's home she entertained family members with her stories. She taught her granddaughters how to make small, tight stitches. She passed her skills on to a new generation.

Betsy missed the bustle of Philadelphia. She made frequent visits back. She would ride the stagecoach into town, see friends and family, go to the Free Quaker Meetings, and then take the stage home.

In 1833, when she was eighty-one years old, Betsy decided to move back to Philadelphia. Her daughter, Jane Canby, welcomed her into her home.

Betsy's eyes gave out completely. She was blind. She rarely left home now. Rocking in her chair with her grandchildren at her feet, she would tell the story of that June day in 1776 when General Washington came to her shop and asked her to make a flag.

BETSY ROSS REMEMBERED

ON JANUARY 30, 1836, BETSY DIED. Her grandson, William Canby, who would tell her story to the world, wrote, "After dinner, we all went in to see her die; and so gently, so like her life, that we could not see that she was not still sleeping."

Seven presidents had held office during Betsy's long life. She had lived through the American Revolution and seen the American victory. She had survived three husbands, two of them sacrificed to the cause of freedom. She had successfully run her own business for fifty years.

She had seen the original thirteen stars of her flag grow in number. There were twenty-five states in the Union when Betsy died—twenty-five stars on the flag.

Betsy Griscom Ross Ashburn Claypoole was buried beside John Claypoole in the graveyard of the Free Quakers just a few blocks from her home on Arch Street. Later, John and Betsy were reburied at 239 Arch Street, the site of the Betsy Ross House.

Betsy's home on Arch Street was preserved through the efforts of many people. Several people owned it after Betsy lived there. In 1891, Charles H. Weisgerber, an artist, began work to save the house in Betsy's memory. To raise money, he painted a picture of Betsy meeting with General Washington. This picture quickly became popular. Mr. Weisgerber then began the movement that led to the creation of the Betsy Ross Memorial Association, which bought the house. Girls and boys around America gave their dimes to help save the historic house.

Betsy's home is now one of the most popular historic sites in Philadelphia. Each year thousands of people visit the Betsy Ross House. They walk up the narrow steps to her bedroom. They gaze at the parlor

In 1893, money was raised to purchase Betsy Ross's house on Arch Street. The house was opened to the public in 1895.

fireplace with its blue tiles, just as it was when Betsy lived there.

Every day and night an American flag, now with fifty stars, flies there in honor of Betsy's contributions to the birth of the United States of America.

CHRONOLOGY

1752   Born on January 1 in Philadelphia, Pennsylvania.

1773   Marries John Ross.
       Boston Tea Party happens in Boston.

1774   Expelled from Quakers and joins Christ Church.
       First Continental Congress meets in Carpenters'
       Hall built by Betsy's father.

1775   Britain declares war on its thirteen American
       colonies.

1776   Betsy's husband, John Ross, dies in an explosion.
       A committee of George Washington, Robert
       Morris, and Colonel George Ross supposedly
       meet with Betsy and ask her to make flag.

1776   July 4—Declaration of Independence signed.

1777   June 14—Congress approves the flag of the
       United States. Betsy Ross marries Joseph
       Ashburn. Betsy Ross is now Elizabeth Griscom
       Ross Ashburn. British occupy Philadelphia. The
       Ashburns will have two daughters.

1777–78 American army winters at Valley Forge.

1781   General Washington defeats Lord Cornwallis at
       Yorktown. The war is almost over.

1782   Betsy learns that her husband, Joseph Ashburn,
       has died in prison in England.

1783   American Revolution is officially over. Treaty
        signed with Great Britain in which Great Britain
        recognizes the independence of the United States.
        Elizabeth Ross Ashburn marries John Claypoole.
        Betsy Ross is now Elizabeth Griscom Ross
        Ashburn Claypoole. They will have five
        daughters.

1789   George Washington is elected first president of
        the United States.

1812   War again with Great Britain.

1817   Betsy's husband, John Claypoole, dies.

1827   Betsy retires from her upholstery and flag-making
        business.

1836   Betsy dies in Philadelphia on January 30.

1870   Grandson William J. Canby tells Betsy Ross's
        story at the Historical Society of Pennsylvania.

BIBLIOGRAPHY

Primary Sources

Canby, William. *The History of the Flag of the United States.*
Document in the Archives of the Historical Society of
Pennsylvania, c.1870.

Drinker, Elizabeth. *The Diary of Elizabeth Drinker, The Life Cycle
of an Eighteenth Century Woman.* Edited by Elaine Crane.
Boston: Northeastern University Press, 1994.

Franklin, Benjamin. *The Autobiography of Benjamin Franklin.*
New York: Washington Square Press, 1972.

Paine, Thomas. *Common Sense.* Mineola, New York: Dover
Publications, 1997.

Washington, George. *Writings.* New York: Literary Classics of
the United States, 1997.

Secondary Sources

Bridenbaugh, Carl, and Jessica Bridenbaugh. *Rebels and
Gentlemen: Philadelphia in the Age of Franklin.* New York:
Reynal and Hitchcock, 1942.

Cooke, Edward S. *Upholstery in America and Europe from the
Seventeenth Century to World War I.* New York: W. W. Norton
and Co., 1987.

Earle, Alice Morse. *Home Life in Colonial Days.* New York:
Macmillan, 1898.

Jackson, John W. *With the British Army in Philadelphia, 1777–
1778.* San Rafael, CA: Presidio Press.

Johnson, Gerald. *Pattern For Liberty, The Story of Old
Philadelphia.* New York: McGraw-Hill Co., 1952.

Lee, Susan and John. *Philadelphia.* Chicago: Children's Press,
1975.

Parry, Edwin S. *Betsy Ross, Quaker Rebel*. Chicago: John C. Winston Co., 1930.

Morris, Robert. *The Truth about Betsy Ross*. Beach Haven, New Jersey: Wynnehaven Publishing, 1982.

————. *The Truth about the American Flag*. Beach Haven, New Jersey: Wynnehaven Publishing, 1976.

Quaife, Milo; Meig, Melvin; and Appleman, Roy. *The History of the United States Flag*. New York: Harper and Row Publishers, 1961.

Tunis, Edwin. *Colonial Living*. New York: Thomas Y. Crowell Company, 1957.

Waldron, William H. *Flags of America*. Huntington, West Virginia: Standard Printing, 1935.

Weigley, Russell F., ed. *Philadelphia: A 300 Year History*. New York: W. W. Norton, 1982.

FURTHER READING

Cobblestone Magazine: The Quakers. December, 1995

Miller, Susan Martins. *Betsy Ross, American Patriot*. Philadelphia: Chelsea House Publishers, 2000.

St. George, Judith. *Betsy Ross: Patriot of Philadelphia*. New York: Henry Holt and Co., 1997.

Wallner, Alexandra. *Betsy Ross*. New York, Holiday House, 1994.

Weil, Ann. *Betsy Ross, Designer of our Flag*. New York, Simon and Schuster, 1986.

FOR MORE INFORMATION

American Flag House and Betsy Ross Memorial
Take a look at the house where Betsy lived and worked for more than a decade. The Web site contains a virtual tour of the house, as well as all the information you will need if you want to visit in person.

(239 Arch Street, Philadelphia, PA 19107)
Phone: (215) 627-5343

Web site: www.ushistory.org/betsy/flaghome.html

Independence National Historical Park Visitor Center
Located in the downtown section of Philadelphia, the visitor center of this park is an excellent place to start if you'd like to visit the locations listed in this book. You can see and learn about the Liberty Bell, Independence Hall, Carpenters' Hall, Christ Church, and other famous historic sites in Philadelphia. The Web site provides excellent tourist information and maps of the area.

(Corner of 3rd Street and Chestnut Street, Philadelphia, PA 19106)
Phone: (215) 597-8974

Web site: www.nps.gov/inde/

PHOTO CREDITS

INDEX

Bold numbers refer to photographs